AF265463

How To Make Love To A Woman

Drew McPherson

ISBN: 978-0-9782441-3-2

Contents

Introduction 7

1. Foreplay 9

2. Oral Sex (cunnilingus) 14

3. Intercourse 21

4. Afterglow 29

Puzzle 32

Introduction

Making proper love to a woman is a lot like enjoying a fine dining experience. It is not a race to see who can finish first. Each bite is to be savoured thoroughly as if it were an entire meal unto itself.

Proper manners require paying close attention to your dining partner so that you finish at the same time and neither feels rushed nor bored with any particular aspect of the full experience.

All details should be a stimulating creative combination that is unlike previous experiences and contains unique and novel sensations, but within an established framework. With practice, this seemingly complex sequence of creative expressions can flow freely as if second nature, and you can become a profoundly deep lover who gives a dynamic and fully satisfying experience to your partner each and every time you come together for a banquet of lovemaking.

There are four main components to a complete lovemaking session. Foreplay, oral sex, intercourse and afterglow. Each has certain tricks and treats which will be explored thoroughly in separate sections to follow:

1. Foreplay

Something most men don't realize is that foreplay begins long before the clothes come off or even before entering the bedroom (or kitchen, living room or wherever you end up going at it). In fact, foreplay can and technically does begin as soon as you enter into communication with a woman.

It can last hours or even sometimes days, months or years. It is a vital part of the build-up to sensational sex.

Ideally by the time the act is about to begin, your partner will literally be quivering with intense tingles of desire and you will have to exercise significant self-control to keep the pace slow enough that you both can enjoy the full experience for a while.

Communication is the key with all aspects of lovemaking. Pay attention to your partner and really try to feel her perspective.

Touch her in places that you might not even consider to be erotic, like her elbows, the inside of her arms just below her armpit, her sides just above her ribs, the back of her knees, her hands and feet.

Gradually work up to more highly erogenous zones, like the nape of her neck, lips, thighs and the small of her back.

Unlike a man who finds it irresistible when a woman goes straight for his cock like a hoover vacuum on overdrive, a woman enjoys a slower, more complete build-up.

While you work your way around her body and explore all of her various sensory areas, notice how she responds. Remember places that make her relax, go limp, quiver or spasm with tingly delight and incorporate those zones into other aspects of your session.

As the loving aspects of foreplay become a customary habit, you will tend to practice them in subtle ways everywhere you go with your lover.

She may be perusing the broccoli at the grocery store when you surprise her with some gentle caresses in just the right places in just the special ways that she loves.

Do this in such a sneaky way that it is a special secret between the two of you that melts her butter. It will start off a tingly vibration. Take time to amplify it and nurture the feeling throughout the day.

Try being playfully seductive with smirky glances and soft touches and suggestive hints. Ideally, this will culminate into mind-blowing orgasms later on that night.

Eye contact is a vitally important part of the entire experience, as is auditory acknowledgement. The sights and sounds of pleasure mutually enhance one's entire existence.

In ideal relationships, lovemaking never truly has a beginning or end, it simply ebbs and flows to different levels and is expressed in different ways.

The concept of foreplay is merely a term describing the waxing phase of a long gradual build-up towards orgasmic release.

Remember this at all times for a more fulfilling and completely connected love life.

2. Oral Sex (cunnilingus)

If there is only one thing you know about how to give good oral sex, it should be that if you thoroughly enjoy the act, your woman will sense and amplify this. Oh, and for heaven's sake, clip your fingernails!

Don't just focus on one part of her vagina. Taste her clitoris, her labia, all around and even inside her vagina. Try different techniques, like broad licks or pointy flicks of the tongue and even suckling gently on various parts.

Always pay close attention to whether she likes or dislikes what you are doing. With time you will learn all of her secrets.

Something most girls really like is having their vagina/clit licked/sucked while you slowly and carefully insert one or two fingers and feel around for her G-spot. It will be a couple of knuckles in and up towards her belly. It is usually a rough little bump about the size of a quarter.

Once you locate it, try rubbing it gently while you are eating her out. Try different amounts of pressure on it and different motions like back and forth, circles or pushing on it and releasing.

When she becomes comfortable enough with her sexuality and is highly aroused you can make her squirt by doing this.

She will initially feel like she has to pee and might be a bit disturbed by the sensation of fluid flowing through her the first time you do this to her.

Reassure her, it is not urine she is feeling, but rather orgasmic fluids.

Once she relaxes into it, there will be waves of increasingly intense pleasure wash over her up to the build-up of full ejaculatory release. Massaging the G-spot a little harder just before and as she starts squirting usually helps. Then let go of it and sort of milk it as if you are squishing the last drops of pee or cum from your penis. It is pretty much the same concept and she will love you for it, especially since this is something very difficult for her to achieve on her own. This manoeuver is called the "Venus Butterfly".

Once you have a good idea where her G spot can be found, remember it for later when you are engaging in full penetration intercourse. There are some clever tips and tricks you can use.

While it may be difficult at first, try to caress your woman along her body while performing oral sex. Especially when receiving oral sex from her, be loving and touch her softly, on her face, her hair, her body, her breasts and nipples.

Let your loving touches mirror your own pleasures as she sucks you off. This will improve communication, helping you both to become better lovers, it will show your appreciation and will get her even more turned on and raring for the next segment of your conjugation.

One important point often missed by inexperienced lovers is that the whole point of lovemaking is to make a game out of it.

The word fore-PLAY says it quite well. It should be fun and tantalizing and last long enough to be satisfying. Many strata should be reached and a breadth of exploration keeps it interesting.

Don't be too goal-oriented. A game that ends immediately is no fun.

Play around with the many different sensations. When you feel yourself or your partner building toward climax, slow down a little and see how long you can remain on the verge.

Feel the ultimate orgasmic anticipation coursing through your veins. Every nerve impulse firing simultaneously, filling your entire perceptual experience with a deep and intense whirlwind of mutual pleasure.

Drink in the unique look, feel, smell and taste of each other. Let

loose with sounds of extreme
pleasure and listen intently to your
partner's sighs and moans.

3. Intercourse

By the time you get to the actual intercourse, you and your partner should be so built up with heated passion that you can barely think straight. Remember, God gave man both a brain and a penis, but only enough blood to run one at a time.

Even though your partner is dripping wet and quivering with desire, don't just ram your rod into her like you are cleaning a chimney. Take your time about it.

Make the act of putting it in take 10 minutes. Tease her a little, first by rubbing your rock hard head on her clit and around her labia. Make her so ravenous for you to be inside her that she tries to forcefully pull you all the way in or begs to be fucked.

Do it gradually. Slip just the head in for a bit then ease it back out. Keep inching your way inside her, feeling more and more of her hot, juicy insides with each mini stroke. Look deep into her eyes with each insertion to see and sense her desire and pleasure intermingled.

This is the point when you need to remember where her G-spot was located and angle your cock to press and grind against it. As you find it and are sliding your head across it, flex the muscles that cause your buttocks to clench. This will cause the head of your penis to inflate fully, expanding to maximum size.

You will need to practice this muscle clenching regularly in order to strengthen your male Kegels to be able to do this most effectively.

Feeling an intense pulse right on her G-spot will be such an intensely pleasurable surprise for her. Look for her eyes to widen and her pupils to roll back into her head.

Try kissing her neck as you do this, pinch a nipple and lick your thumb and rub it across her clit simultaneously and see how she reacts.

It is important to vary your technique to keep it interesting and give your partner pleasant little surprises. Don't just be a mindless jackhammer.

Pay attention to her whole body and notice how she reacts, feel her emotions and pleasures. Take your time. Slow down when you feel her building towards climax. Let the pleasure build more deeply. You both have plenty of time to thoroughly enjoy it. Every nuance and slight variation. Really grind your cock inside her. Plunge in with abandon to feel every nook and cranny, every ridge and ripple.

Explore your partner, touch her, kiss her, feel her – make **love** to her.

She may have several orgasms by the time you are ready to pour yourself into her. If you have spent enough time to build up a massive load, this will be ideal.

Simultaneous orgasm will come naturally as you become fully in tune with each other and feedback off one another's pleasures and tingles.

It is important to fully let yourself go when you achieve release.

Make sure your partner knows that she is free to fully unleash the wild beast inside of her. If she feels the irresistible urge to let loose a powerful moan, claw into you and suck every last drop of you into her with wild, rhythmic pelvic spasms then encourage her to do so. Releasing your own primal urges, let out a guttural grunt and fully go into the haze and feel it for all that it is.

Merge with your partner in the common artistic expression of transferring your seed from deep inside you, all the way up inside of her. The deeper the better, on both accounts.

Don't force your orgasm. Let it build on its own and when you are finishing, go limp, let your body react of its own accord. Don't exercise any control whatsoever.

You will find that if you both release control, then the intimacy and connection will take over. Your pleasure will be enhanced by magnitudes.

Synergy occurs when you can feel not just your own pleasures and tingles but those of your partner as well.

Though it will be difficult not to be dragged over the edge, try to remain in that ultimate tantric state with her as long as possible.

As you both get good at it, you will slow right down to the point that you are experiencing intense pleasure and connection by barely moving. Your orgasmic juices will have built up so much that they

actually start flowing out of you
long before climax actually occurs.

You could get to the point where
your mutual orgasm lasts longer
than the total duration of some
people's entire sexual repertoire.

4. Afterglow

Continued intimacy after climax is an often underrated part of the total lovemaking package.

As the oxytocin is welling up inside you, get really close and partake in some tender touching. Soft, gentle caresses and sweet loving kisses will finish the experience nicely.

This brings you together with a chemical reinforcement. The sacred bond is fortified.

Thus begins the next phase of the continuous cycle of intimacy. It connects seamlessly to the upcoming phase of foreplay.

You may find yourself becoming so aroused during the afterglow cuddles that you cannot contain yourself. Several sessions of lovemaking may result all in the same night. Maybe even spanning several days.

The tender moments shared after sex are a key component of the bonding experience of falling and re-falling into love. A long-lasting couple fall in love not just once, but each and every time a lovemaking session wraps up in the afterglow phase.

Communication and openness during this phase will be at a maximum. It's a good time to muse about future hopes and dreams, be